Myths and Legends of
The
WOLF

Abigail Frost
Illustrated by Francis Phillipps

MARSHALL CAVENDISH
New York · London · Toronto · Sydney

Library Edition Published 1990

Published by Marshall Cavendish Corporation
147 West Merrick Road
Freeport, Long Island
N.Y. 11520

Library edition produced by DPM
Printed by Colorcraft Ltd. in Hong Kong.

Adapted by AS Publishing from La Chevalerie, published by Hachette.

Library of Congress Cataloging-in-Publication Data

Frost, Abigail.

The Wolf / by Abigail Frost.
  p. cm. - (Myths and legends)
Includes index
  Summary: A collection of Creation myths, classical and Norse myths, and legends and traditional stories from Europe and other areas of the world, all concerning the wolf.
  ISBN 1-85435-237-7 (lib. bdg.)
  [1. Wolves-Religious aspects-Juvenile literature. 2. Wolves-Folklore. 3. Mythology. 4. Folklore.] I. Title. II. Series: Frost, Abigail, Myths and legends.
  BL443.W6F76 1990
398.24'52974442-dc20   89-17445
                                                           CIP
                                                           AC

▷ CONTENTS ◁

THE CREATION OF WOLVES

For centuries, people have feared wolves and told stories about them, depicting them as evil creatures that prey on the innocent. The story of the wolf's creation, like many of those that follow, is a traditional tale. It links the wolf with the Bible story of God's creation of Adam and Eve and portrays wolf and woman alike as dangerous.

After God banished Adam and Eve from the Garden of Eden, he felt sorry for them. "Maybe I was too harsh," he told himself. "I had to punish their disobedience, but after living in Paradise, how will they cope with hunger and cold?" He wanted to make their lives happier. He had an idea and called Adam and Eve.

They expected more punishment. Adam looked anxiously at a willow-rod which God held out to him. But God said gently, "When you are hungry, and can find nothing to eat, strike this rod upon the sea!"

Then God whispered to Adam, warning him to not to let Eve use the rod.

Just as God expected, Adam and Eve found life outside Paradise hard. Soon they had nothing to eat. So they went to the seashore, and Adam struck the sea three times with the mysterious rod. A pure white animal walked out of the sea and rubbed its soft fleece on Adam's leg. "Eve," said Adam, "Here is a sheep, which will give us milk and cheese."

Greedy Eve wanted another sheep. When Adam slept, she took the rod and struck the sea. A dark creature rose up, its face cruel and its mouth full of sharp fangs; a fierce and monstrous wolf! With a roar, it grabbed the poor sheep and dragged it into a wood. Eve's screams woke Adam. He seized the rod and struck the sea with all his might.

"Alas! Another wolf!" he cried, as a new animal emerged from the waters, big as the wild beast before. It ran to the wood where the sheep had gone – and brought it back!

The sheep was still shaking from its terrible ordeal, but it was safe and sound. The new animal lay down at their feet, with love in its eyes. This was no wolf. "It's a dog!" said Adam. "He will be our faithful companion."

Adam and Eve used the rod again many times. They discovered that the animals Adam called up were easy to tame, while those that Eve summoned from the sea soon ran off to the forest, where they lived a wild life.

Adam's animals were tame, but Eve's were wild.

THE ISLAND OF WOLVES

In Greece, there lived a princess called Theophane, who was as beautiful as a goddess. Many suitors came and endeavored to please her, but she was in no hurry to choose a husband. All these young men around her father's palace made life amusing. But sometimes she wanted peace. So she would go with her maids to the seashore. They went in the morning, before her suitors got up. Alone on the beach, the girls took off their clothes and splashed in the water, laughing joyously.

Poseidon, the sea-god, lived under the water in a shining palace. Sometimes he came up from the depths in his chariot, drawn by fiery horses with golden manes. He whipped up the waters with his trident, so that the waves frothed around him. The god was invisible to humans; only the tempests he raised made his presence known.

One morning, Poseidon saw Theophane on the beach and fell in love with the beautiful princess. Jealous of her suitors, the god decided to take her away from them.

Next morning, a great wave snatched Theophane from the beach. Her helpless maids watched as she was carried out to sea; she seemed to fly on the waves, then disappear over the horizon in a flurry of foam. . .

At the palace, sorrow soon gave way to anger. The suitors guessed that Poseidon was to blame. By consulting oracles and magicians, they learned that the god was hiding Theophane on an island in the Aegean Sea. All rivalry forgotten, they sailed together in search of her, ready to brave every storm the god might send.

After many tempestuous days at sea, the suitors landed on the island. They broke up into little groups to search every corner. But

6

they had to admit defeat; they found nothing on the island but hundreds of sheep! No people, not even a shepherd! All the houses were deserted. Where were their owners?

One frustrated suitor took his spear and killed a peacefully grazing sheep. The others followed his lead. Then they gathered wood for a fire, and flayed and gutted the sheep ready to roast.

A little way away, on top of a hill, a huge ram stood watching the scene. At his side was a spotless white ewe. Suddenly the ram reared up

Each young man saw his friend become a wolf – and realized it was happening to him!

on his hind legs; his hoofs came down in a shower of sparks. At that moment, lightning flashed from his horns to the beach, where the men, drunk with blood and rage, were feasting on roast mutton. One cried out in horror, as he saw his friends fall on all fours, covered with dark hair. He felt his own ears grow longer, and his body change. All the suitors were losing human shape. They tried to speak, but could only howl. They had become wolves!

Now the beach was full of puzzled wolves. The ram and the beautiful ewe took back their true shapes – Poseidon and Theophane. They had become sheep as a disguise and turned the islanders into sheep as well. Furious at the young men's behavior, Poseidon condemned them to stay as wolves for the rest of their lives.

Nobody has ever found the island where Poseidon hid Theophane. And her suitors were never seen again. Perhaps, somewhere in the Aegean Sea, there is still an island inhabited only by wolves.

▷ APOLLO'S CHOICE ◁

The jealous Greek goddess Hera was furious at her husband Zeus's unfaithfulness. She forbade the earth to give her rival any place to sleep. The unhappy girl, whose name was Leto, had to leave her home in the far north, where the god Boreas blew icy winds. Poor Leto wandered from place to place with angry Hera close behind. She was chased from cities, islands and even deserts. At last, she took refuge in a deep forest. Afraid of wild animals, she took the form of a she-wolf.

In wolf's guise, Leto found a place Hera had overlooked, a little wandering island which was not fixed to the bottom of the sea. There Leto gave birth to twins; the goddess Artemis, and the god Apollo.

Leto's troubles were not over. She took her babies to Lycia, "land of wolves," but shepherds there threw stones at them to chase them away. In revenge, she turned them into frogs and brought up her children in peace.

Zeus gave his son Apollo a lyre, and he became god of music. He grew up radiantly beautiful, and many nymphs fell in love with him. Among them was Cyrene, a huntress who guarded her father's herds against wild animals in the forest. When Apollo saw her, Cyrene was being attacked by a lion. The god took wolf's shape and drove the lion away. Then he took back his own shape and carried her off in his chariot.

On the mainland of Greece, at Delphi, Apollo killed the monster Python which lived in a cave on Mount Parnassus and terrorized the inhabitants. The grateful citizens built him a temple. Pilgrims from miles around brought offerings to the god, and soon the temple had a store of treasure. One day, a thief took it all.

A wolf howled all night outside Delphi. The people thought it was a sign from the god. They followed it to a wood on the mountain-peak,

Leto disguised herself as a wolf.

8

where they found the stolen treasure and the thief's body. In gratitude, they erected a bronze statue of a wolf next to the statue of Apollo.

A crowd of curious people stood by the harbor in the Greek city of Argos, as they did whenever a ship arrived. This one was magnificent. It had fifty oarsmen, twenty-five on each side. It must have been built for long and perilous journeys. The crowd waited impatiently for the sailors to disembark, eager to question them: "Who are you? Where are you from?"

Imagine their surprise when they saw that the "oarsmen" were young girls! Dumbstruck, they let the girls pass. The only man on the mysterious ship seemed to be the captain. He addressed the astonished crowd: "My name is Danaus, and these are my fifty daughters. I have crossed the sea pursued by my fifty nephews and my brother Aegyptus, king of Egypt. Take me to your leader!"

King Gelanor, who ruled Argos, welcomed the new arrival – who thanked him by saying he intended to become king in his place! Gelanor was displeased of course, but it was the custom of his country for the people to choose their leader. So he organized a public debate.

Both candidates spoke long and eloquently, but the people of Argos could not decide. Many preferred Gelanor, whom they knew, while Danaus was a stranger, newly arrived the previous day. At dawn, a crowd gathered in the town square to hear the last debate. As the speeches began, there was a cry of alarm from some shepherds. A wolf had left the forest and attacked a herd of cattle outside the town. It had killed the bull!

The Greeks believed in omens, and they took this event for one. The god Apollo was a friend of the wolves. They compared the wolf's sudden arrival to Danaus's. They decided he was the god's choice and made him king. In gratitude, he built a great temple to Apollo, god of wolves.

The wolf had killed the bull!

▷ THE MARBLE WOLF ◁

Phocus, son of King Aeacus and the sea-nymph Psamathe, had won all the prizes at the Games. His beaten half-brothers, Telamon and Peleus, complained jealously afterward.

Telamon grumbled as his slave massaged him: "It's always the same! Phocus always wins! This must stop!" Peleus, rubbing his body with perfumed oil, silently agreed.

Next day, as the three athletes were training, Telamon threw a stone at Phocus's head. He fell down dead. The brothers hid the body and returned to the palace.

Aeacus sent soldiers to search for his missing son. They quickly found the corpse and the culprits too. Everyone knew they were jealous, and no one believed their story that it was an accident. The king sadly banished his sons. Watched by their angry stepmother, Psamathe, they went to seek their fortunes separately.

Peleus, who had to leave behind his lovely wife and his son, Achilles, was sorry about his part in the crime. When he reached the kingdom of Trachinia, he decided not to say why he had been exiled. Leaving his herd of oxen outside the town, Peleus asked the king if he could stay. "Your name is famous," said the king, "Make this your home."

One hot day, the herdsman led Peleus's oxen to the seashore, near a temple dedicated to the sea-god Nereus and his daughters, the Nereids. Among the Nereids were Psamathe, Peleus's stepmother, and his wife, Thetis. As the oxen entered the cool water, a great wolf attacked them, its mouth red with blood. Some shepherds who tried to save them met the same fate. The terrified herdsman ran to find Peleus.

The Nereid takes her vengeance.

10

The king of Trachinia at once ordered his men to arms. He wanted to lead them himself, but his wife begged him not to risk his life. Peleus explained, "This wolf has come against me alone, because I have wronged a Nereid! Let me ask her for mercy!"

The king and Peleus climbed to the top of a lighthouse that overlooked the shore and saw the monstrous wolf killing its prey. Peleus stretched out his hands to the sea, begging his stepmother to stop, but she was deaf to his prayers.

The wild beast ravened on. Peleus called his wife Thetis: "Sea-goddess, ask your sister for her pardon!" At last, Psamathe took pity and tried to call the wolf off, but it would not obey. As it bit another victim's neck, the angry goddess turned it to marble. For years to come, the shepherds feared that menacing marble wolf on the beach.

▷ THE RIVER'S GIFT ◁

At dawn, the wolf left his lair on the side of the hill. He sniffed the wind with ears pricked. As the sun rose higher, shepherds' voices echoed around the Palatine Hill. All was calm, as usual. Silently the wolf moved into the brushwood.

As he vanished, another animal came out; a big she-wolf. From the crags behind came the plaintive cries of her new cubs. Like her mate, the she-wolf made sure there was no danger and then went downhill. She was wary of the people by the river, but she had to go there to drink. She walked quickly, so as not to leave her young ones too long.

She usually had her drink at a reedy spot on the bank where she could not be seen. But this morning something she did not understand made her stop farther away, where the river grew wide and slow. Here, there was a little sandy beach, where women washed linen and children played with driftwood all day. The she-wolf advanced into the open and began to drink. Suddenly the wind brought a new smell; she lifted her head curiously and saw something floating toward her. It was a large basket like those the washerwomen used.

The she-wolf did not flee. The same force which had brought her to this place commanded her to approach the basket, now beached on the sand. She heard little whimpers that reminded her of the cries of her own young ones. Inside the basket was a white cloth – and something moving underneath. Lifting the cloth with her teeth, the wolf saw two human cubs, new-born babies with soft pink skin, sleeping side by side.

The she-wolf felt hungry; but her mothering instinct was stronger. She gently lifted one baby in her mouth and ran back to her lair, dropping it with her cubs. Then she returned to the river and gently took up the other baby. Back in her lair, she lay on her side and offered her milk to the little ones – the human cubs as well as her own.

Her mate returned with a juicy hare at noon. He was not bothered by the new arrivals. Dropping his catch at her feet, he went outside to stand guard.

The she-wolf took care of the babies for several months. All that time, a woodpecker flew around outside the lair. The wolves let it alone; the bird obeyed the same mysterious orders as they did. It watched for danger and brought sweet berries for the little ones. Soon the cubs grew up and went out to hunt, but the babies were not yet able to walk. The she-wolf returned to her hunting life and would disappear for long periods, leaving her adopted babies in the woodpecker's care.

One day, she saw the woodpecker fly up in alarm as she returned. Walking with care, she saw a shepherd, crying out in surprise. Then he bent down and took the two babies in his arms. Knowing she must not interfere, she let him take them away.

Centuries later, a great city stood by the river. Its people honored the she-wolf's memory; a bronze statue showed her obeying the god Mars's orders, feeding the twins she had saved. Their names were Romulus and Remus. Romulus had founded the city which now bears his name – the city of Rome.

The she-wolf tenderly examined the strange cubs she had found.

▷ FENIR THE FIRE-WOLF ◁

The Norse gods met at Odin's palace, Valhalla. Usually, they ate a lavish feast washed down with plenty to drink; but this time they needed to keep clear heads. They were in danger: the wolf Fenir planned to attack their celestial kingdom, Asgard!

Fenir was related to the giants who lived in Asgard when the world was first made. They wanted revenge on the gods who had taken their place. The wolf, son of Loki, spirit of fire, and a giantess, was of monstrous size. One of his jaws touched the sky, the other the earth. He galloped around the universe swallowing everything in his path. The gods had already tried to chain him up on a deserted island.

Then, Fenir had seemed strangely tame as they passed a great steel chain around his neck. They scented victory, but the giant wolf flexed his muscles and broke his metal bonds as if they were straw. The gods had tried a heavier chain, but the wolf broke that too. So now they met again at Valhalla, frustrated by failure.

"Why don't we just kill this evil wolf?" roared Thor, the red-bearded thunder god. "I'll break his skull with one blow of my magic hammer! Then we can have a feast!"

The dwarf blacksmiths did their work in secret.

14

Thor was ravenous, and the lack of food put him in a bad temper. Baldur the Good spoke next: "Calm down, Thor! We must chain Fenir to show that we are the masters."

Odin, the wise god of war, then spoke: "Baldur is right, Thor. Your hammer and my lance would be useless. But you have given me an idea. The dwarf blacksmiths who made our magic weapons can make a chain to bind Fenir. Let's find them at once!"

Like the giants, the dwarves had been conquered by the gods. These ugly little men now lived underground, forging magic weapons for the gods and fine jewelry for the goddesses. They undertook Odin's work in secret.

The master smith, an old dwarf with skin tanned by the forge's heat, delivered the finished article. His eyes glittered as he un-

folded a long ribbon, soft as silk and light as air. "Here is a chain that cannot be broken!"

The gods passed the silky sash from hand to hand, tugging at it, ever harder. Even Thor's great muscles could not break it. Convinced, the gods asked the smith what it was. "This ribbon is made by a secret process," he said. "Six things are in it: a cat's meow, a woman's beard, the roots of the mountains, a bear's tendons, a fish's breath and a bird's spittle."

▷ TYR'S SACRIFICE ◁

The gods thanked him and went to meet Fenir on the lonely island of Armwartner. The great wolf had been suspicious for some time. The gods had been taking too much notice of him.

When they arrived for the third time, Fenir was wary; he pretended to sleep, but glanced through half-closed eyes at his visitors. Fenir feared Odin most of all, because he had the power to see the future. The wolf knew he must take them by surprise. The gods approached talking cheerfully, and when they were nearby, the wolf pretended to wake. He gave a great yawn which revealed his sharpened fangs.

"Good day, Fenir!" said Odin. "Would you like to play with us?"

Careful! What are they after? thought the wolf. Aloud, he growled "Let's see."

"See this ribbon?" said Odin. "We have all tried to break it, but even Thor has failed. Some of us say even you couldn't do it. Others say that you alone have the strength. Will you show us what you can do?"

The giant wolf shook with rage. "It's a trap!" he thought, but if he refused the challenge, he would seem a coward. He thought fast and answered, keeping his calm:

"Very well, I accept your challenge, but on one condition. When you tie the ribbon, one of you must put his hand in my jaws."

Silently, Fenir watched the gods' reaction. Odin lowered his head to hide his grim face under the big hat he always wore. Thor clenched his magic hammer, unable to hide his rage. Thor's wife, Frig, went pale and Freya,

Odin's wife, nervously twisted her fine gold necklace. Only Baldur was calm.

The great wolf was triumphant. The gods had indeed tried to trick him, and now they were on the defensive. Fenir stood up, ready to crush his enemies with all his weight.

Then one of the gods came forward: Tyr, a warrior respected in battle for his valor, his honor and his wisdom. Modestly, he had stood aside, and Fenir had not noticed him.

When the wolf saw Tyr, he was alarmed, though he pretended not to be. "I'm not afraid," he said to himself, "No god has enough courage to sacrifice his hand." But Tyr, silent and untrembling, held out his right hand before the monster's mouth. Fenir's jaws opened . . .

Powerful hands held down the beast and tied fast the magic ribbon. Then the gods cautiously withdrew, all except Tyr, who stayed to keep his bargain with Fenir.

The wolf tried to move, puffing up his chest to break his bonds – in vain. His mighty paws could not break the ribbon. Frothing with rage, he heard the gods laugh at their beaten foe. But one did not laugh. Tyr stood by his side with quiet dignity. Slowly, Fenir closed his jaws, but Tyr did not move his hand. Then the wolf's fangs snapped shut and severed Tyr's wrist.

Fenir had lost the game. The gods, relieved, congratulated their brave volunteer. Tyr's sacrifice had made up for the dishonesty of their trick. The great wolf howled in his chains. Before they left, one of the gods thrust his sword through the wolf's jaws to stifle his howls.

Brave Tyr keeps his word to the wolf.

▷ TWILIGHT OF THE GODS ◁

Long ages passed. Asgard was surrounded by thick, menacing snow-clouds. Cold and shadows reigned over all the world, for Fenir's two wolf-children, who eternally chased the sun and the moon, had succeeded in eating them up. Blasts of wind had torn up all the trees and whipped up floods, and the uproar of the storm rose to Asgard.

Odin recognized these signs: they heralded the last battle between gods and giants. The giants had plotted their revenge through the dark days and nights. Now they were ready to attack.

Changing his big hat for a battle helmet,

Odin sharpened his magic lance and called his personal guard to order. These fearsome warriors came to Odin eager to fight, their shoulders hung with the skins of wolves and bears they had slain.

Then Odin called all the gods of Asgard together at Valhalla to tell them the news: "The hour of the great battle is near. Fenir, the fire-wolf, has managed to free himself, and so has his wicked father, Loki, the spirit of fire, whom we had bound hand and foot to stop him from doing harm. They are leading the giants' army. A ship full of ghost-warriors is sailing toward us from the kingdom of the dead. Get

ready for war, for we must face them all together."

As he spoke, Odin turned to his son, Thor, who had fought giants many times before. The evil creatures feared his terrible hammer.

The gods waited for the moment of confrontation. Whirlwinds of snow swept the air. Mountains collapsed, forcing the dwarf blacksmiths from their underground homes.

At last one day, the golden-crested rooster which perched on the walls of Valhalla crowed aloud: another replied from the kingdom of the dead. These roosters were destined to crow only once in their lives – to announce when the battle was to start. Heimdall sounded the alarm. The hour had come. The gods marched toward the battlefield. Odin, who led them, knew how the battle would end.

The last battle between gods, giants and monsters.

19

▷ MORTAL COMBAT ◁

A sinister shape loomed out of the thick fog in the west: Naglfar, the ship of Hell, built from dead men's nails. Between the wild and rolling waves, the monstrous jaws of its living dragon prow could be seen. At the helm of the ghost ship stood the giant Hrymr, lifting his glittering shield in defiance. The Midgard serpent, whose body circled the earth, raised a tempest, furiously twisting its massive body and whipping the waves with its tail. The air and the sea were fouled with its venomous breath. As Hrymr stepped ashore, a gigantic tidal wave arose, destroying everything in its path.

Between the two camps was a vast plain a thousand leagues across. The air was full of angry roars and the clash of arms. Already, under the raging elements unchained by the giants' fury, the landscape looked like the end of the world.

Suddenly to the south, a blinding flash of lightning streaked across the sky, as the fire giants galloped past on their sweating horses. Their leader Sutr wheeled around in front, brandishing a sword brighter than the sun. Flames burst out under his horse's shoes and in his wake the earth tore itself apart in great cracks. Faster and faster, the fire giants drove their steeds toward the citadel of the gods. As the last fiery horse left the rainbow which linked Asgard to the earth, it burst into flames. Then the celestial city collapsed into a shower of sparks.

Now the gods and the giants were face to face, and in an instant they were upon each other. In the midst of his warriors, Odin sought his foe: the wolf Fenir! It had been prophesied that they must fight. And there was the ravening wild beast, which sprang with gaping mouth, his breath on fire; flames spattered from his eyes and nostrils as he let out a menacing howl. No wolf had ever seemed more deadly!

Fearlessly, Odin threw himself on the giant beast, which grasped him between his jaws, leaving him no chance to fight. The prophecy which said that the wolf would be the death of the leader of the gods had come true. But the battle was not over. . .

Before the wolf had finished his meal, Odin's son Vidar closed his jaws with a violent kick; then he pushed into Fenir's mouth a sword so long that it penetrated the wolf's heart.

The fierce battle raged on and on, until all the gods and all the giants had killed each other. Humans in their turn disappeared from the now uninhabitable earth, annihilated by the fires, earthquakes and tidal waves which devastated all. A rain of stars fell from the sky, and the darkening earth perished in the floods.

The prophecy comes true – Odin faces the wolf.

BROTHER WOLF

The people of Gubbio dared not leave the little Italian town. At night, they cowered in their houses, timidly hiding in bed until dawn drove out their fear. By day, they braved the narrow streets to meet and talk. The subject was always the latest ravages of the wolf.

For some time, a huge wolf had terrorized their land. Nobody dared work in the fields. The animals were confined to their stables and pens, the crops rotted underfoot and the countryside grew more desolate each day. Gubbio seemed like a town under siege; the people huddled behind its walls. Cut off from the world outside, they feared they would soon starve to death. Several times, a band of men had gone to hunt the wolf, but each time they had failed. The men lost courage, and the women prayed to God to rescue them.

Nearby, in Assisi, lived a man who charmed the animals by his gentle manner and his smile alone. He had dedicated himself to Jesus Christ, and he brought hope and happiness to the poor and unhappy. When he heard of the wolf of Gubbio, he decided that he must free the townspeople from their misery and fear. The man's name was Francis Bernardone, but everyone knew him as Brother Francis. He lived in poverty with his followers, whom he called his brothers, or friars.

Francis and a friar took the road to Gubbio. They went barefoot, wearing simple robes of heavy cloth. All the way, Francis sang hymns to the creator of the natural world. The people of the town welcomed him warmly, but asked themselves how, short of a miracle, this mild-looking man could save them from the savage wolf. When Francis wanted to go unarmed, with only the friar for company, they thought they were talking to a madman! But Francis steadfastly made them open the town gate. As the two frail figures disappeared into the

St. Francis was the friend of all wild creatures.

countryside, the women of Gubbio fell to their knees, praying for the safety of these saintly men.

Singing to the glory of God, Francis took the road to the forest where the wolf had his den. His frightened companion recited prayer after prayer, hardly daring to take breath. Suddenly, he heard a howl. Struck dumb with fear, the poor friar hid behind a rock, while Francis turned bravely toward the wolf's voice. . .

The wolf stood in the middle of the path, lips drawn back ready to spring. But it was puzzled; the man did not flee, he walked forward. The bloodthirsty beast hesitated for a moment and Francis spoke:

"Brother Wolf, you have disobeyed our Saviour by killing his creatures without permission. In Christ's name, I command you to do no more harm to me or anyone else."

Francis loved all the creatures of the earth. He often talked to his friends, the birds. But would his simple words tame this savage beast?

Just a few steps separated man and wolf. The wolf walked toward Francis, who stood still. When it reached him, the wolf stopped. It sat obediently at the holy man's feet, giving him a paw in submission.

When the townspeople saw the two brothers return with the wolf trotting at their side like a pet dog, they did not believe their eyes. They did not believe their ears either, when Francis asked them to give the wolf food, since it would never again harm them. But he persuaded them, and so the fearsome wolf of Gubbio lived peacefully in the little town, going from door to door to collect its daily rations.

The wolf collects his daily rations.

▷ THE DEVIL'S CONTRACT ◁

Sightseers thronged the masons' yard at Aix-la-Chapelle in France. People loved to watch the carpenters, stonemasons and carvers at work on a great cathedral. Young apprentices tried to learn the old craftsmen's secrets. Members of the city council came to check how the work was progressing.

The work had taken many years, for a cathedral is not built in a day. The proud city fathers wanted the finest cathedral in France. So they spared no expense and hired the very best craftsmen. But as the years passed, the costs mounted up. City officials visited the yard with anxious faces; soon, there would be no money left!

Then, one day, a rich traveler came to the city's best inn. He galloped into town on a black horse, attended by a black-coated groom, who spoke a language nobody could recognize. The master spoke perfect French. He asked for the biggest room and ordered the rarest meats. He tipped the staff well and they rushed to serve him.

Like all visitors, the stranger went to see the cathedral and took great interest in every detail. He looked over the plans and talked with the craftsmen as knowledgeably as one of their own trade. Then suddenly he went back to the inn without another word. Soon the man and his wealth were the talk of the town. Had he not told the innkeeper that the cathedral would be the "most beautiful monument in the world?"

"How proud the people of Aix will be!" he kept saying.

But the hard-pressed city fathers announced that the work must stop. The whole town was upset at the news. But what could be done? The city was too deep in debt to carry on. One morning, the traveler went to the city hall and offered the assembly a fabulous sum – enough gold to finish the cathedral. "We can never repay you!" they said, but the officials' eyes gleamed with foolish hope.

"There is no question of repayment," replied the stranger icily. "I ask only one insignificant thing in exchange: the soul of the first worshipper to enter the cathedral. You see, it's nothing!"

The city fathers grew pale with fear; the stranger was the Devil! All was explained, the black horse, the strange groom, the bottomless purse! Was it too late to chase him out of town?

But the Devil had sown envy into the hearts of the townspeople, and the majority was in favor of accepting the bargain: one soul, they said, that wasn't much. No one thought the soul would be his own!

Thanks to the Devil's gold, the finished cathedral was even finer than expected. The Devil left town and was almost forgotten – until the day when the cathedral was to be consecrated. No one wanted to go in!

A crowd gathered in the square outside. "There are the officials who signed the contract," they muttered, "Let one of them give his soul to the Devil!"

Suddenly, a man stepped forward, carrying a big sack. Low growls could be heard from it. He walked to the cathedral porch. "He must be mad! Or is he a saint?" cried the people. On the porch the man half-opened the door, then placed his sack on the ground and slid it inside. Then he kicked the sack, crying: "Take this, Devil!" The people in the square saw a bushy tail disappear into the dark nave and cheered.

Alone beneath the high cathedral vault, the wolf shuddered. It was a prisoner in a stone forest. Its human enemies had given its soul to the Devil.

Trapped!

THE WEREWOLF'S TALE

The young mistress of the castle was the envy of all. Her husband was a fine young knight and a great friend of the king. But she was unhappy. Each week, her husband fell into deep melancholy and disappeared for three whole days. No one knew what became of him, but when he returned, he was in a joyful mood, as though relieved of a great burden.

At last, his lady dared to speak about it. "Sire," she said nervously, "if you love me, rid me of this terrible anxiety. Tell me what happens when you go away!"

The knight looked at her sadly and refused to answer. This only made her more curious, and she asked again. Finally, the trembling knight revealed the truth:

"Madam," he said, "Do you know what Bisclavert means? Turnskin! That's what we call werewolves in my homeland, Brittany. I am a turnskin! Each week I must go to the forest and live like a wild animal!"

The lady knew her husband was under a curse. He answered all her questions save one. He refused to say where he hid his clothes in the forest. "If I lost them, I would have to remain a wolf for the rest of my life!" But his wife insisted, saying he must trust her. The knight gave in again:

"I hide them under a hollow stone near an old chapel in the forest, by a crossroads."

The knight was glad to have shared his sad secret. But he had lost his lady's love. Frightened, she wanted to be rid of him.

Later the knight went to the forest as usual, but did not return after three days. Servants and soldiers searched in vain. They sadly grew to believe their lord was dead. The lady married another man, a lord who had loved her for many years.

The knight grew hairy and could only howl.

26

One day, the king went hunting in the forest. The hounds found a huge wolf and chased it eagerly. Hours later, the exhausted wolf surrendered; it turned around to face the king and began to lick his leg.

"See this miracle!" said the king. "The beast asks for mercy like a man! I shall grant it – call off the hounds!"

Then he rode off, but the wolf followed him, as if it were one of the king's men. The king kept the animal as a pet.

The courtiers grew used to the friendly wolf. But one day it seemed to show its old wild self. The king had invited all his lords to court. Suddenly, the wolf jumped on one lord and bit him viciously, to the astonishment of all. Shortly afterward, the wolf attacked a lady, biting off her nose. The king's wisest minister said:

"Sire, this wolf would not bite without a good reason. The lady it bit was the wife of your friend, the knight who vanished last year; the lord it attacked is her second husband. Let us question the lady!"

The lady soon confessed. She had made her lover take her husband's clothes from their hiding place under the hollow stone. Her husband had to stay in the forest, doomed to remain a wolf.

The king realized that his pet was his old friend. He sent for the clothes and gave them to the wolf. But nothing happened. "Put the wolf in a room with the clothes," said the minister, "and leave it alone."

A little later, the king entered the room and saw his friend, the knight, asleep in bed. His wicked wife was banished – and all her daughters were born with no noses!

The friendly wolf turns savage.

▷ THREE SILVER BULLETS ◁

Once a year, at the end of May, the priest led all the people of the village in procession to bless the fields, asking God to give them good crops and protect their lands from drought and hail.

Little Mary walked in front, as pleased as punch. She was nine years old, just old enough to understand the importance of the ceremony. Dressed in her best, she carried a cross of flowers to place in her parents' fields. She had made the cross herself and chosen where to leave it: a tiny patch at the end of the path, by a little wood, which her father had sown with corn. How happy he would be if this, his first crop, were fruitful!

Mary hurried along, but the others moved more slowly. It was hot, and the elderly priest was tired. Behind him, his parishioners quietly chatted, and children gathered wild berries from the hedgerow.

Lost in her own thoughts, Mary walked on far ahead of the procession. As she entered the little wood, a breeze chilled her, so she threw her pretty new flowered shawl over her shoulders. Then she sat down on a tree-stump and waited for the others.

The priest led the people in a prayer, but suddenly the murmuring of the villagers was drowned by a howl. They saw a wolf streak across the path dragging something in its jaws. Then they noticed that Mary was missing. . .

They followed the beast's tracks into the wood, but found only the child's cross of flowers and her new shawl. The angry villagers wanted revenge.

30

Night and day three thousand peasants tracked the creature, armed with scythes, axes and forks. "Vengeance!" they cried, but to no avail. They saw the monstrous beast's sinister shadow many times, but never could they catch it. Soon word went around that it had come from Hell – sent by Satan to bring them sorrow.

One night, old Father Martin who lived a little way out of the village was woken by a sudden noise. Peeping from his door he saw a gigantic animal, half-wolf, half-woman, creeping around his chicken-run. The poor man lost his mind. A little later, some frightened children said they had been chased by a huge beast, which sometimes ran like a wolf and sometimes leaped like a goat. This devil-wolf could change itself at will!

One man, the caretaker at a nearby monastery, swore to kill the beast. Like all the able-bodied men in the district, he had many times gone out in search of the wolf. Every day, his anger grew. He did not like to fail, and he felt it was his mission to destroy the creature from Hell.

Buried in his garden were three silver coins, his savings for his old age. He dug them up and melted them down to make silver bullets – the only thing which could kill a wolf from hell. On each bullet, he carved a cross, took them to the priest for a blessing and went to find his quarry.

They met in a dark hollow. At first he could see only two red eyes glowing in the dark. Then the animal's shape grew clear. The two stood still, face to face.

The caretaker raised his rifle and fired – on target. The beast staggered back several steps. It let out a dying howl which froze its foe with fear. The villagers found its remains hundreds of yards from the road. At first, no one dared approach the body. The wolf was dead, but the caretaker had suffered such terror that his hair turned white overnight.

A terrible end to the procession.

▷ THE WOLVES' CROSSROADS ◁

It was unlucky to stop at a crossroads at night. Witches, ghosts or the Devil himself might snare the careless traveler. In France, at a crossroads in a wood in Brittany, there was one night of the year when you could see a strange gathering.

Yves was returning from an evening at old Mrs. Soizic's. She was the best storyteller for miles. He had listened to her tales attentively, eating pancakes washed down with sparkling cider. He left arm in arm with other boys and girls; but, one after the other, his friends reached their houses. Yves, who lived farther away in a cottage on the other side of a wood, walked alone under the full moon.

The old woman's stories kept running through his mind, especially one about dark spirits which trapped unwary travelers. Ghostly shadows flitted between the trees and he could hear strange noises. Desperate to get home, he

A strange meeting by moonlight.

decided to take a short cut – through the wood.

The path through the wood grew darker, until it reached a broad clearing where three more paths met. At this crossroads was a huge oak tree, hundreds of years old. "What a bad idea!" he cried to himself. "I should have gone around this wood." Then he heard leaves rustling in the thickets and thought he was being watched. He picked up a stone and gripped his stick firmly. The clearing ahead was bright with moonlight; the oak's shadow cast fantastic shapes on the ground. Suddenly a gray shape crossed the light; Yves saw its red eyes and long thick tongue. "A wolf!" Quickly he removed his shoes, hoping to bang them together to frighten the beast away. But now another shadow, and a third appeared. Jumping back into his shoes, Yves quickly climbed a tree.

A huge number of wolves had taken possession of the clearing, singly or in groups. Quietly, they sat down, forming a vast circle around the oak tree. At the foot of the tree stood a big black wolf with a proud look. He waited perfectly still while his brothers took their places, then lifted his head to the moon and gave a long howl which froze Yves to the bone. There were more surprises and terrors in store for the poor boy. The wolf stopped howling and began to speak like a man:

"Wolf-people, we are gathered together as we do every year to chose our new king. Each pack-leader must come in turn to the tree and tell us his deeds for the year; our king will be the most deserving."

Yves listened in horror at their stories of sheep ripped open, of horses killed. . . He recognized some from the night's fireside tales. Most of the wolves had killed only animals, but one crazed-looking wolf boasted of having feasted on human flesh. He said it was his favorite food! But the others hardly listened, and he moved off grumpily. Yves, clinging to his branch, hardly dared to breathe.

The place under the oak was taken by group of some 15 wolves, who sat in close ranks.

"We obey one man, a great sorcerer." announced one. "He dictates when we attack. Under his protection, we are all stronger."

"A wolf leader!" murmured Yves, realizing why some herds in the district were attacked more than others.

The election took place amid terrific howling and the meeting was called to a close. Day broke over the deserted clearing. Heavy-headed and stiff, Yves went on his way. He had heard so many horrible tales that he could no longer remember even that of the new wolf-king, who had taken the gruesome name of "King of Sheep." Had he been dreaming? Maybe – but he had a good story for the next evening at old Mrs. Soizic's.

In search of the dreaded Beast.

THE BEAST OF GEVAUDAN

The Beast saw a tiny figure tramping along the path. Silently it waited, its eyes gleaming. The little girl did not see the Beast as it leapt upon her, too swift and powerful for her to fight back. Jeanne Boulet was 14 years old in that year, 1764, and lived in the mountains of Gévaudan, in France. When the villagers found her half eaten corpse, they blamed wolves which were common in the area. "Take care," they told their children. "Never linger in the woods."

Sadly, more children were killed, and people began to wonder if mere wolves could slaughter so many. Had some fearsome new creature

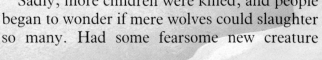

arrived in the mountains? One September day the Beast attacked a woman beside her home. Her neighbors drove it away, but the poor woman was dead. "What was the creature like?" friends asked the people who had seen it.

"It is huge and dark. . . and it is quick! It flew off like an arrow! It is a creature like no other!"

"Look, footprints!" cried one man in a trembling voice. Everyone shivered with fear. These huge prints were not wolf-tracks!

All witnesses agreed; this Beast was a diabolically cunning creature. It never attacked grown men, but went for women and children. Hunters went after it and killed more than 70 wolves. One was enormous, and nearly black; but was it the guilty Beast? Alas, no, for the Beast soon returned.

One day, however, the Beast was wounded as it attacked a young boy. It took flight and people thought they were rid of it. But some time later, it jumped on an old man at the well. Brave washerwomen working nearby beat the Beast instead of their linen and it ran away. "It's a monster," they said, "as big as a year-old bull!"

More stories flew around. Somebody had seen the Beast walking upright on its back legs like a man! Others had heard it laughing! It could leap ten yards! One man had caught it leaning on his window sill!

A sad Christmas approached, marking six months of the Beast's reign of terror. There was now a price on its head: the king and the local bishop offered a huge reward to its killer. But it escaped from every trap. At last, the army was called. But the soldiers were almost as unpopular as the Beast: they had to be housed and fed, their horses too. And the captain put anyone who did not help them in prison.

"We're a laughing-stock!" complained the peasants. "How can we kill the Beast when we aren't allowed to carry guns? We're only good enough to be beaters! And who'll get the reward? Some rich stranger."

"This Beast can only be killed by bullets blessed by a priest," some said.

One Sunday after mass, people gathered outside the church. The bishop had said that God had sent the Beast to punish the wicked! The Catholics blamed the Protestants, and the Protestants blamed the Catholics. People were frightened and despairing. The Beast's ill-deeds continued . . .

▷ THE CHILDREN'S BATTLE ◁

As the New Year began, the Beast was still on the prowl. It had killed another woman. Everywhere, its huge prints were found in the snow.

Soon it was time for the farm animals to go out into the fields. Tending them was the children's job, but with the Beast around they had to be careful. "Stay together," their parents said, "and stay high up where you can see it coming!" Each boy had a long stick with a knife-blade attached to it.

The little battalion marched off with the animals. Their captain, the oldest boy, cheered on the rest: "Come on, quick march! Close ranks! Never fear; the Beast's not here!"

"This is how I'll kill the Beast!" said a smaller boy, poking an imaginary foe with his bayonet. "Take that!" They all laughed, except for one little girl. She said: "First make the sign of the cross! The Beast is the Devil and you know what the priest says – if you see the Devil, cross yourself at once!"

At the top of the mountain, they let the animals go off to feed, while they went to gather firewood. It was cold, and besides, a fire might

The children beat the Beast!

scare off the Beast. In a thicket, they came face to face with the Beast! They had not heard it arrive. The children regrouped, with the biggest in front, holding their bayonets out. The Beast began to circle them, to attack from behind; but the children turned with it. Then it grabbed the smallest boy and dragged him off.

"Courage! Don't run off! Kill it! Kill it!" cried the captain to his friends. Their weapons slid off its thick fur. At last, they made it put down its victim – whose cheek was badly torn. There was no time to draw breath; the Beast came straight back at them and took another boy. All hope seemed lost.

"Quick!" cried the captain. "We'll surround it!" The plan worked; the Beast fell into some mud, and the children trapped it.

"Go for its eyes!" ordered the captain, determined to save his friend. The Beast, busy fending them off, held the boy tight, but did not bite him. At last, the captain drove it off with a last desperate blow. The boy ran free, and the children had won. With a savage howl, the Beast vanished into the undergrowth.

37

▷ A MYSTERIOUS GAMEKEEPER ◁

The Beast must have recovered, for it was still around in February; it avoided all the villagers' traps and escaped every danger. How could they beat such an enemy? Nobody had discovered its den or found out anything about its daily habits.

The army captain stationed in the town hoped to surprise it. He made his men follow the children, armed to the teeth, but dressed in women's clothes to fool the Beast. His stupid plan failed, and the soldiers went away, a laughing-stock.

A hunter from Normandy called d'Enneval and his son replaced them. They spared no effort to track the Beast, going on foot through thick snow. Hope returned on April 23, when they killed a huge she-wolf – whose stomach contained pieces of clothing. Some thought that at last they were rid of the nightmare; but the hunters were not so sure. They seemed pre-occupied by a mystery which they refused to explain. Soon the Beast struck again: on May 24, the day of the spring fair, it killed three times in two hours!

Mr. d'Enneval doggedly continued his search. He concentrated his efforts on a lonely village on the bare mountain heights. "It's a witches' village," said some locals – adding that the Devil himself had once lived there. A good place to seek the Beast? But it wasn't. In June the Beast was seen nearby, but it escaped the hounds after attacking two women. "It must be

Antoine was a strange man – could he be a wolf-charmer?

hiding in the woods!" said Mr. d'Enneval, "But why did the hounds lose its scent? Something must be masking it!"

Antoine Chastel, gamekeeper in the woods, was a strange man who lived apart from others. For many years, he had wandered abroad and had only recently returned to the area. Where had he been? Strange stories went around: some said he had been taken prisoner by pirates who had taken him to Arabia, where he had learned to charm wild beasts – wolves, perhaps? Since his return, he had spoken to nobody but his old parents. Mr. d'Enneval tried to meet this mysterious man. but he did not get the chance. The king recalled him and his son.

In their place, the king sent his rifleman Antoine de Beauterne, with 15 royal gamekeepers and wolfhounds. In three months they never once saw the Beast! Had some sixth sense – or a charmer – told it of danger?

But Antoine de Beauterne refused to give up. He would not go away without the promised reward. On September 25, 1765, he shot a huge wolf – and declared that it was the Beast. He sent its skin to the king's palace at Versailles, where sightseers came to gasp and shiver at it, and he pocketed the reward.

But in Gévaudan, no one dared believe the miracle; and with good reason. The attacks returned at the year's end, more violent than before.

On June 19, 1767, three hundred men went hunting in the woods. If the Beast was there, it could not escape. Jean Chastel, the father of the mysterious gamekeeper, loaded his gun with bullets which the priest had blessed. He fired the shot that killed the Beast. The animal was a wolf, but it was a gigantic and exceptionally strong one. For many years no grass would grow on the spot where the Beast fell dead.

39

▷ THE WOLVES' STORM ◁

It had been a hot and humid week; the people and animals were tired. After the cooler early hours of the day, people sought the shade of their farms; in the fields, the animals huddled under trees, away from the sweltering sun. There was no sound or movement in the countryside. Only the hot air vibrated above the stony roads, threatening.

The year was 1603, and the place a village in the Jura mountains. One night, thick clouds built up in the west and hid the sun. They swelled up like huge mushrooms and rolled over the overheated sky. Night came early, and the treetops began to bend under the first gusts of wind.

A violent storm broke. The wind tore branches from the trees with loud crashes; hailstones flattened crops, covering the fields in a thick white carpet. Blinding lightning bolts ripped the sky, followed by the heavy crack of thunder. A ball of fire rolled over a hay-rick and huge red flames lit up the darkness – where demons from Hell seemed to dance.

Then the storm died down, as quickly as it had risen. One by one the doors opened, and anxious farmers stood on their steps, as though they had woken from nightmares.

The damage was spectacular; trees in the orchard were bent and broken and the fruit crop was ruined. "Dear Lord! What have we done to deserve this?" murmured some. Others said: "It's the work of a demon!"

40

Visitors from Hell?

The air was still charged with electricity. The moon had risen, but its pale light hardly pierced the thick fog which now covered the fields, giving everything a white halo. People stayed close to their houses, not daring to explore the changed landscape.

Then they saw three gray silhouettes, slipping slowly past like shadow puppets against the curtain of fog . . . three big wolves, walking single file, to who could tell what destination? Was it a hallucination, brought on by the shock of the storm? A sudden break in the fog dispelled their doubts; the animals were there, all right – fierce, silent and sinister. They passed among the herds of goats, cows, sheep, but did not touch them. Only the last wolf seemed to hesitate; taking a step back, it went up to a kid which was frozen with fear. Seizing the shivering creature in its jaws, it dragged it a little way, then dropped it, unharmed.

Seeing this strange behavior, the people were more frightened still:

"Look how their eyes glow!" said one to his neighbor. "Werewolves! They must be werewolves!" said another, his voice choked with fear. "Oh God!" moaned a woman, crossing herself. A child began to cry, but was silenced with a slap. Everyone was silent, holding their breath.

The creatures walked across the devastated fields and back again, several times.

"You'd think they were inspecting the damage!" said one man angrily. "As if they were proud of it! I think they're witches who have brought the storm to ruin us!"

Now everyone was convinced that the storm was the work of a demonic power. The leading wolf, they thought, must be the Devil himself! They all knew he liked to take the form of a wolf to terrorize humans . . .

WOLF MYTHS AND LEGENDS

1 Wolf society
The mountain people of Georgia, now part of the U.S.S.R., once thought wolves had a society just like people. They were under the protection of a saint and were not thought of as wild animals. Hunters who killed a wolf wore mourning clothes as if they had killed a man.

2 Guardians of Valhalla
When Odin sat on his throne in the palace of Valhalla, two great wolves sat at his feet and ate up the remains of the gods' great feasts. Their names were Geri Gobble-guts and Freki Swallow-up.

3 Sons of the gray wolf
The Turks and the Mongols of old were enemies; but they both claimed to be descended from wolves. One young Turkish warrior, who alone survived after a Mongol raid, was rescued by a she-wolf and led by her to a secret earthly paradise in the mountains. They were married, and their children were led by a great gray wolf to the land which is now Turkey. The Mongol emperor Genghis Khan also claimed to be the son of a wolf.

4 The wolf in the sky
In ancient China, people believed that eclipses of the sun were caused by a great sky-wolf eating up the sun. People beat drums and shot arrows at the sun to drive the animal away.

5 Lycaon
Lycaon was the first king of Arcadia in Greece. He led a wicked life. The god Zeus came in disguise to a banquet at his palace and was disgusted to be served a child's limbs. The god destroyed the palace and turned the king and his sons into wolves. Then he sent a flood to drown them all.

6 The Egyptian wolf-god
The Egyptians had a wolf god, Wepwawet, whose name meant "he who opens the road." He led kings in battle, and his image was carried through the streets of his town, Assiut, during a great annual festival.

7 Wolves and the church
One old legend says that Jesus made a wolf keep hungry goats out of his mother's garden. Many saints tamed wolves, just as St. Francis of Assisi did. In Brittany, a blind saint called Hervé made a wolf which had killed his dog guide him around. St. Austreberthe, a medieval abbot, had a donkey which was killed by a wolf. He made the wolf carry his washing to the water!

8 The lucky wolf
The Romans thought it lucky to see a wolf. The animal was sacred to Mars, god of war and protector of Rome. Julius Caesar's victory over the Gauls at Sentinium, in 195 B.C., was attributed to a wolf which was sent by Mars to frighten the enemy.

Why are there so many stories about wolves? They have always fascinated people. Their glowing eyes which pierce the night, their dawn hunts, their sharp teeth, their mournful night-time howls – these have inspired legends and superstitions from the dawn of time. Wolves have their place in history just as they do in mythology.

Wolves and war

Warrior peoples admired the wolf's power and cunning. Some of the Gauls, Celtic tribes whom Julius Caesar fought, covered their helmets with a wolf's head, symbol of their manly strength. The wolf, along with the horse, the eagle and the wild boar, was one of the emblems of Roman legions. The German Nibelungen legend tells how warriors used to eat roast wolf-meat to give themselves the courage of a wolf. In Scandinavian myths, which are all about valor, wolves have an important place, showing how they inspire fascination and fear in fighting men. When Odin, god of war and of wisdom, sat on his throne, two great tame wolves lay at his feet, the symbol of his power. But the giant wolf Fenir represents destruction and violence.

The Roman god Mars, who sent a she-wolf to help Romulus and Remus, was the protector of the city of Rome which Romulus founded. Mars was god of war and the protector of nature and of youth. Each year in March – the month which bears his name – a great festival took place in the towns near Rome to thank the god for the new spring. During these festivities, young people were selected to leave their homes and seek their fortunes abroad. When they left their town, they were guided by two animals sacred to Mars, the woodpecker and the wolf. Spring was also the season when soldiers left their winter quarters to begin new campaigns. Mars and the wolf were their protectors.

The wolf is often associated with war long after Roman times. A knightly

The she-wolf suckles Romulus and Remus. Her foster child's city is HEAD OF THE WORLD.

order called the Order of the Wolf was founded in the 1400s. From the Middle Ages to the time of the French Revolution, the people of Bruyères, in Picardy, formed a militia to defend the freedom of their community. They proudly called themselves the wolves of Bruyères. Nearer our own times, the German soldiers who occupied much of Europe in World War II were often compared to wolves.

The link between wolves and the young survives in the name of the Wolf Cubs, the branch of the British Boy Scouts for younger boys. Sir Robert Baden-Powell, the British soldier who founded the Scouts, named the Wolf Cubs after Rudyard Kipling's stories about Mowgli, a little Indian boy who was brought up by wolves.

Superstitions

More and more the wolf became a cursed beast instead of the lucky creature it had been for the Greeks and Romans. In the last century, many fishermen believed it was unlucky to mention a wolf on board ship; if someone did, they turned back quickly for fear of being wrecked. Some people believed that the breath and flesh of a wolf were poisonous, because of the snakes and vermin it had eaten.

In some places, people practiced magic to protect themselves from wolves, nailing wolves' feet to stable doors to drive others away. Sometimes they even hung a dead wolf from a tree. Shepherds recited wolf-prayers, spells to keep the wolves away from their flocks. Others would actually sacrifice a lamb each year by throwing it to a wolf, hoping that this gift would satisfy it.

One superstition where the wolf remained lucky was the custom of using its teeth as a charm to keep away nightmares.

Witches and werewolves

From keeping wolves away with spells, it was a short step to trying to control them by magic. French country people believed that some people, called wolf-charmers, could tame these savage creatures. It was important to keep on the right side of a wolf-charmer, or he might send his wolves to get your sheep. These so-called charmers were usually charcoal-burners, or solitary shepherds, who lived outside the villages. When the Beast of Gévaudan frightened the peasants in the 1700s, they thought that Antoine Chastel, a strange and lonely man, was a wolf-charmer.

In reality, wolves do not take well to

Symbols of war and peace: the wolf and the lamb.

Wolf-charmers could even ride their devilish subjects.

captivity. There are a few in zoos, but the only performing wolves ever known were used in Roman circuses, for cruel and bloody battles with bears.

Werewolves frightened people far more than the real animals. They were men believed to be condemned to wander at night in the form of wolves, often on the night of the full moon. To be cured, they had to admit to the crime which had led to this punishment and to be wounded by a silver – or a blessed – bullet.

Hollywood brought the legend of the werewolf to a new audience in the 1930s, in a series of films starring Lon Chaney, Jr. Chaney played the werewolf as a sad and gentle man, who hated the violent life he led as a wolf; rather like the medieval Breton werewolf, Bisclavert.

The wolf and light

The wolf is a night animal, and therefore seems mysterious. But because of its eyes, which appear almost luminous, it was often associated with the worship of light and of the sun. The ancient Egyptians believed their ancestors were guided to the country by a wolf-god, Wepwawet. He also guided the sun-god's barge during its voyage over the night sky.

In Greece, wolves were sacred to the sun-god Apollo and were offered to him as sacrifices. The god was thought to have met wolves during his winter stay in the far regions of the north. For these Mediterranean people, the wolf suggested, not bright light, but the cold of the night and of winter.

In the early Greek language, the words for light (*luke*) and for wolf (*lykos*) were so close that they became confused: Apollo Lycius was a name for the sun-god which suggested a god of light and a god of wolves. A similar example is the Gauls' god of light, Belen or Belonus, whose name comes from *bleis*, which meant wolf in the Celtic languages.

The cursed wolf

The most common theme in wolf legends is the wolf as the enemy of people and livestock. In Europe, wolves and bears were the most dangerous wild beasts; but being more numerous, wolves were more feared.

Arcadian shepherds in ancient Greece

A 15th-century engraving of a wolf-man.

honored the hunt-goddess Artemis, and often called her "Wolf-killer," asking her to protect the herds. Mount Lycia, named for the many wolves on its wooded slopes, was in this area. The legend of Lycaon, the mythical king who was turned into a wolf by Zeus, comes from here.

For the Jews, the wolf was a living sign of God's power. God sent the "desert wolf" to citizens of Jerusalem who refused to convert to Judaism. Later the Christian church adopted the same idea. In the 1700s, Catholic priests stated that the Beast which terrorized Gévaudan had been sent by God to punish the people for their wickedness.

But the country people were more likely to think wolves were sent by the Devil. The wolf was the shepherd's worst enemy; and Jesus Christ was often described as the good shepherd, looking after the people, his flock. So the wolf came to represent the Devil. Medieval actors in religious plays wore wolf-skins to portray the Devil.

Some Christian stories show wolves in a better light. An Anglo-Saxon monk wrote about how a wolf protected a saint's head from his enemies. When pagan Danes killed St. Edmund, the Christian king of East Anglia in 870, they cut off his head and threw it into the bushes. His followers searched for it, guided by the head's own cries of "Here, here, here." At last, it was found in the thickest part of the forest, guarded by a fierce wolf, which willingly gave up the head to Edmund's friends.

Wolves and illness

The werewolf legend may have some basis in fact. A disease called porphyria, which affects the human mind and body, can produce roughness in the skin which might look a little like hair, and a cramping of the muscles which makes people bend as if walking on all fours. Its victims are sometimes unable to endure sunlight, so that they tend to live by night. On some sad occasions, mentally-ill people have believed themselves to be werewolves and acted in a similar way. There was a case in the British town of Southampton in 1987.

One terrible disease which wolves can carry is rabies, which is associated with "mad dogs," but can affect any mammal, including humans and wolves. It is spread by bites, and its effects are terrible, unless the person who has caught it is vaccinated very quickly. Some countries, such as Britain and Ireland, stay rabies-free by imposing long quarantines on imported animals, including pets.

A rabid wolf, in great pain, would lose its usual fear of humans and attack any creature which approached it. Before it died, it could easily infect several dozen people and animals. This was a real fear; before Louis Pasteur discovered a vaccine in 1885, a long and agonizing death was the inevitable result of a bite from a rabid animal.

Once wolves were hunted as vermin and for sport.

Hunters rounded up wolves by leaving deer as "bait."

Wolf-hunts

The kings of medieval Europe loved to hunt in great style, and wolf-hunting was particularly popular. They appointed courtiers to run wolf-hunts and bred special hounds. Some breeds of dog, such as the Irish Wolfhound, are descendants of these hounds. Later governments (in North America as well as Europe), hoping to eliminate wolves, put a price on their heads; a reward was paid to anyone who could produce proof of killing one.

This system worked (perhaps too well) in Britain, where the wolf was extinct by the mid-1700s. This is one reason why there are fewer wolf-legends found in Britain than on the continent of Europe. Several places are claimed to be the one where the last British wolf was killed; one unlikely candidate (because it is so near London, and wolves prefer lonely places) was Hounslow Heath, site of the present-day Heathrow Airport.

New World wolves

North American Indians brought the animals that lived around them into their tribal myths. Shamans, or medicine men, of the North Pacific coastal tribes performed a dance in wolf-skins to heal the sick. It commemorated how a spirit called Changer killed the wolf-chief and danced in his skin.

The Algonquin-speaking tribes of the Eastern Woodlands told how the Great Hare, Manabush, had a wolf brother, Moqwaio. One day, Moqwaio was walking along a frozen river and evil spirits dragged him down into a hole in the ice, where he drowned. After five days of searching for him, Manabush met his wolf brother's ghost. Manabush told Moqwaio to go to the west and build a great fire there, to guide the souls of the dead to their new home and to keep them warm.

Wolves had some close encounters with white Americans, too. Davy Crockett (died 1836), the Tennessee congressman who was "king of the wild frontier," told voters tall tales about his exploits. Among them was this account of meeting a wolf while resting in a hollow tree: "He stared right up in my

face, as much as to ask leave to pick a breakfast off any part of me he wanted. I was so astonished at his impudence that I stood right still . . . Then the wolf turned around, and was going off, when the end of his tail stuck through a big knot hole in the tree. I ketched hold and pulled his tail through . . . I tied his tail into a big knot and fastened it with a strap, so that he couldn't haul it out, and left him there to amuse himself."

Wolves today

The wolf still lives on in northern and Mediterranean Europe, North America and Siberia, and parts of Asia, but its numbers are much reduced. As the old forests they lived in have been cut down and rail tracks and major roads built,

Wolves are protected species now in many countries.

The nobles hunted on horseback. Their men followed the hounds on foot.

there are fewer places for wolves to live in peace. A few wolves have learned to live close to humans. Some live in garbage dumps near Rome: a sad fate for the animal that fed the city's founder.

Some wild wolves live in the more remote parts of Spain and Yugoslavia, and there are many more in the great forests of North America and the U.S.S.R. In France, the only remaining wolves live in special reservations.

Naturalists studying wolves have presented the animals in a new light. Though wolves kill for food, they never kill needlessly. Most live and hunt in large family groups called packs. Members of the pack are highly social, looking after the cubs and protecting each other. Each pack has a leader which all the others obey. "Lone" wolves have to fend for themselves, and it is they that tend to kill easy targets such as domestic animals.

As people become more aware of the need to protect wildlife, movements devoted to saving wolves in their natural habitat have grown, in Europe, Canada and the U.S. Gradually, we are learning to respect these animals, so long hated and feared.

▷ INDEX ◁